TABLE OF CONTENTS

CHAPTER 1

Pioneers 5

CHAPTER 2

WNBA Stars 13

CHAPTER 3

The Next Wave 25

Milestones ▪ 30

Glossary ▪ 31

To Learn More ▪ 32

Index ▪ 32

LEGENDS OF WOMEN'S BASKETBALL

By Emma Huddleston

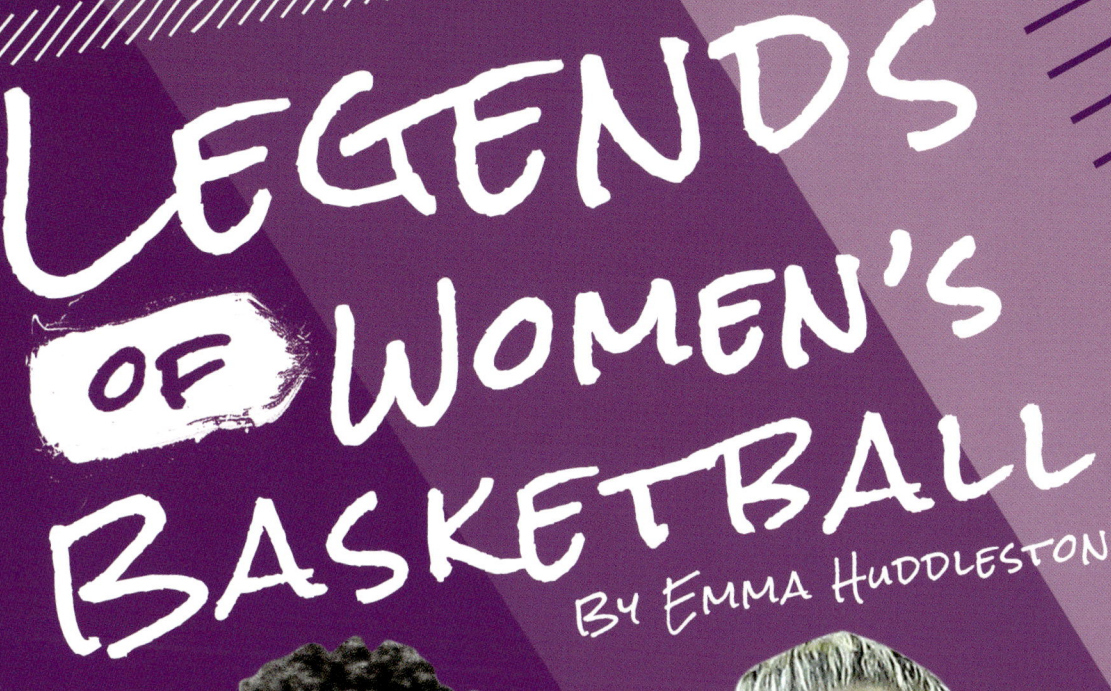

Copyright © 2021 by Press Room Editions. All rights reserved. No part of this book may be used or reproduced in any manner whatsoever, including internet usage, without written permission from the copyright owner, except in the case of brief quotations embodied in critical articles and reviews.

Book design by Sarah Taplin
Cover design by Sarah Taplin

Photographs ©: Dave Tennenbaum/AP Images, cover (left), 1 (left); M. Anthony Nesmith/Icon Sportswire/AP Images, cover (right), 1 (right); AP Images, 4; Alvin Chung/AP Images, 7; Charlie Neibergall/AP Images, 9; Kathy Willens/AP Images, 11; Michael Caulfield/AP Images, 12; Mike Fiala/AP Images, 15; Matt York/AP Images, 17; Anthony Nesmith/Cal Sport Media/AP Images, 19; John Froschauer/AP Images, 20; Stacy Bengs/AP Images, 23; Chris O'Meara/AP Images, 24; Jessica Hill/AP Images, 27; Tony Quinn/Icon Sportswire/AP Images, 29

Press Box Books, an imprint of Press Room Editions.

ISBN
978-1-63494-281-2 (library bound)
978-1-63494-299-7 (paperback)
978-1-63494-335-2 (epub)
978-1-63494-317-8 (hosted ebook)

Library of Congress Control Number: 2020913889

Distributed by North Star Editions, Inc.
2297 Waters Drive
Mendota Heights, MN 55120
www.northstareditions.com

Printed in the United States of America
012021

About the Author
Emma Huddleston lives in Minnesota with her husband. She enjoys writing children's books, running, hiking, and swing dancing. After learning about these legends in women's sports, she hopes young people feel empowered to be the best they can be.

CHAPTER 1

PIONEERS

Nancy Lieberman threw a no-look pass. Her Detroit Shock teammate caught it and scored. For nine minutes that night, Lieberman ran the court. She didn't score, but she dished out another assist as the Shock lost to the Houston Comets.

Typically, there's no reason to notice nine minutes of playing time. But this game was special because Lieberman had come out of retirement at age 50. She had been training for months. Now she was making history. She was the oldest

Nancy Lieberman is the youngest player to win an Olympic medal in basketball for the United States.

woman to play in a Women's National Basketball Association (WNBA) game.

Defying expectations was nothing new for Lieberman. In 1976, she won a silver medal as an 18-year-old on the US Olympic team. Then she led Old Dominion University to two national championships before she turned pro.

Lieberman didn't have any real opportunities to play professionally in the United States until 1997. That year, the WNBA began play. Lieberman was 39. Still, she came out of retirement to play one season. Lieberman was the oldest player to debut in the league. Her brief return 11 years later lasted just one game. But it gave fans another example of why she's one of the legends of the sport.

Cheryl Miller was another player whose career peaked before the WNBA existed. In one

Cheryl Miller dominated the sport during her college years at the University of Southern California (USC).

high school game, she scored 105 of her team's 179 points. That was a national record.

While playing at USC, she won two National Collegiate Athletic Association (NCAA) titles.

Miller also won the tournament's Most Valuable Player (MVP) Award twice.

Her post-college success came with USA Basketball because there weren't women's pro leagues in the US. The 1984 Olympics were held in her hometown of Los Angeles. Team USA played South Korea in the final. Miller scored 16 points and led her team to gold.

Teresa Edwards was one of Miller's US teammates that year. That was the first of five trips to the Olympics for the University of Georgia star. Edwards had come a long way from

COACHING GIANT

Pat Summitt coached the University of Tennessee women's team to eight national titles. She also won an Olympic silver medal as a Team USA player in 1976 and a gold medal as head coach in 1984. Summitt was known for intensity and discipline. She made her players work hard. But it paid off when it mattered most. During her coaching career, Summitt won a record 1,098 games. And in 2012, she received the Presidential Medal of Freedom.

Pat Summitt's University of Tennessee teams won eight national titles.

shooting at a bike rim nailed to a pine tree at her grandmother's house as a kid. She spent most of her pro career playing overseas. But she always came back to play for Team USA. Eventually, Edwards returned to the United States for good, playing in the American Basketball League (ABL). In 2003, she came out of retirement to play for the WNBA's Minnesota Lynx.

Like Edwards, Teresa Weatherspoon had to leave the country to establish herself as a professional. Weatherspoon played point guard at Louisiana Tech University. As a senior in 1988, she led her team to the national title. The same year, Weatherspoon won Olympic gold for Team USA. Then she played eight years in Europe until the WNBA launched in 1997.

Playing for the New York Liberty, the 31-year-old led the new league in assists. She also won the first of two straight Defensive Player of the Year Awards. Weatherspoon was also known for her hustle and intensity. Her years of experience helped her outplay younger, quicker guards.

Point guard Teresa Weatherspoon was a fierce competitor.

In the 1999 WNBA playoffs, Weatherspoon made a desperation half-court shot to give the Liberty a win. That play remains one of the league's most memorable moments.

CHAPTER 2

WNBA STARS

Cynthia Cooper made the game look easy at times. With a flick of her wrist, the basketball would soar through the air and into the hoop. Cooper was known for being able to score from anywhere on the court.

However, after a great college career at USC, the one place she couldn't score from was home. That's because there was no US pro league. Finally, after playing 11 years in Europe, she got her chance. The WNBA tipped off in 1997. At age 34,

Cynthia Cooper drives to the hoop in a 1997 game.

Cooper led the Houston Comets to the first WNBA title—and the next three as well. And she was the Finals MVP all four years.

The Comets were the first dynasty in the small, newly established WNBA. Cooper, Sheryl Swoopes, and Tina Thompson were known as Houston's Big Three. Swoopes was the team's defensive ace. She was named WNBA Defensive Player of the Year three times. Swoopes also become the first female basketball player with her own line of sneakers. Nike released "Air Swoopes" in 1995. When she jumped, people could see an S on the bottom of each shoe.

Thompson couldn't have guessed she would end up on the winningest team of the WNBA.

Sheryl Swoopes, *right*, was a key part of Houston's four straight WNBA titles.

She didn't grow up with professional women's basketball players to look up to. She thought she might become a lawyer. But her skill and passion led to her being the No. 1 pick in the WNBA's first draft. Thompson did whatever it took to win, whether that meant scoring, passing, or rebounding. She played nearly 500 career games in 17 WNBA seasons. She averaged more than 10 points per game in 15 of those seasons.

Lisa Leslie was Thompson's college teammate at USC. She was used to making history. In high school, she once scored 101 points in the first half of a game. Later, Leslie became the first woman to dunk in a WNBA game. She was one of the early faces of the

Lisa Leslie was one of the first stars in the WNBA.

league and won two titles and three league MVP awards with the Los Angeles Sparks.

Leslie and Indiana Fever legend Tamika Catchings each won four Olympic gold medals with Team USA. Catchings also was named to the all-WNBA first or second team 12 times in 15 years. Catchings was known as one of the league's most competitive players. That grit and determination was on display as she led the Fever to the 2012 WNBA title.

Late in the deciding game of the Finals, the Fever led the Minnesota Lynx by nine points. The game was all but over, but Catchings kept playing tough defense until the buzzer sounded. That was the only way she knew how to play.

Tamika Catchings sets up for a three-pointer during the 2012 WNBA playoffs.

Lauren Jackson, *left*, and Sue Bird had plenty of opportunities to celebrate with the Seattle Storm.

Catchings retired as the WNBA career leader in steals with 1,074. That's 300 more than the player in second place.

Like many great players, Lauren Jackson seemed destined to play basketball. Both her parents played for Australia's national teams.

Jackson was just 20 years old when she made her WNBA debut with the Seattle Storm in 2001. The 6'6" forward was difficult to guard. When opponents tried crowding her in the lane, she would back them down and shoot over them. If they gave her too much space, she would step back and drain a jump shot. Jackson led the WNBA in scoring three times. She's also fifth all-time with 586 blocked shots through 2020.

Jackson and point guard Sue Bird led the Storm to WNBA titles in 2004 and 2010. Bird won two NCAA titles and a national Player of the Year Award at the University of Connecticut (UConn). Then she became a legend in Seattle.

Bird holds the all-time WNBA record for assists. But skilled passes are just one part of what makes a great point guard. Bird also averaged double figures in points in each of her first 16 WNBA seasons. She led the Storm to another title in 2018 at age 37.

Diana Taurasi was one of Bird's teammates in college. She also became one of the sport's most consistent winners. Taurasi won three national titles at UConn before joining the Phoenix Mercury. Then she won three WNBA championships. Brash and confident, Taurasi never shied away from a tough shot or a tough defender. Through 2020,

SOCIAL JUSTICE

Maya Moore showed basketball skills from a young age. She only lost three games in high school. In 2011, Moore was the WNBA's first draft pick and Rookie of the Year. She went on to win four league titles with the Minnesota Lynx. She chose to step away from the game in 2019 to dedicate her time and money to fix flaws in the nation's justice system. In 2020, she helped win freedom for a Black man who had been wrongfully imprisoned.

Diana Taurasi, *left*, keeps a close eye on Maya Moore during the 2013 WNBA playoffs.

she had scored nearly 1,500 more points than any player in WNBA history.

CHAPTER 3

THE NEXT WAVE

The Seattle Storm were on fire in the 2018 WNBA Finals, thanks to one of their young stars. Forward Breanna Stewart, the league MVP, was making layups, jumpers, and three-pointers look easy all night.

In the final minute of the last game, she cut across the court. Teammate Sue Bird passed her the ball. Stewart made a final layup, and the Storm won. Stewart was named the Finals MVP. And she was just 24 years old.

Breanna Stewart shoots over an opponent in a 2020 game.

Brittney Griner is one of Stewart's top rivals. The Phoenix Mercury center is one of the best shot-blockers in the game. One night in 2014, Griner caused major problems for the Tulsa Shock. By the end of the night, she had rejected 11 shots. That set a record for most blocked shots in a WNBA game.

Griner was dominant in college ball at Baylor and was the first pick when she joined the WNBA in 2013. She dunked twice in her professional debut. During the next three seasons, she totaled more than 300 blocks.

Elena Delle Donne was named the WNBA Rookie of Year in 2013. She became the first WNBA player in the 50-40-90 club in 2019. Those numbers are her shooting percentages for field goals, three-pointers, and free throws.

Few players have much success when they drive to the basket against Brittney Griner (42).

Topping all three of those numbers in one season is a rare feat.

Delle Donne is an effective shooter because of her 6'5" frame and eye for the basket. In 2019, she won the league MVP award playing for the Washington Mystics. Their potent offense averaged a league-record 113 points per 100 possessions. Delle Donne also led the Mystics to the team's first WNBA title.

The New York Liberty made Sabrina Ionescu the No. 1 pick of the 2020 WNBA Draft. At the University of Oregon, the flashy point guard was known for posting triple doubles while playing amazing defense. In February 2020, she made

STAR SISTERS
The Ogwumike sisters, Nneka and Chiney, starred at Stanford University. Nneka, who is two years older, was the WNBA MVP and won the league title with the Los Angeles Sparks in 2016. Chiney became Stanford's career leading scorer before being drafted by the Connecticut Sun in 2014. Five years later she was traded to Los Angeles and reunited with her sister.

Elena Delle Donne takes the ball to the hoop against the Connecticut Sun in 2018.

NCAA history as the first college player, male or female, to reach 2,000 points, 1,000 assists, and 1,000 rebounds. The WNBA is counting on Ionescu and other young players to lead the league to a bright future.

MILESTONES

1893
The first college women's basketball game is held at Smith College.

1970
Women's basketball starts using five-player, full-court rules.

1976
Women's basketball becomes an Olympic sport.

1978
The Women's Basketball League begins its three-year run as the only professional women's basketball league in the United States.

1996
Sheryl Swoopes is the first player to sign with the WNBA.

2000
Teresa Edwards becomes the first woman to play in five Olympics and win five medals.

2016
Team USA wins Olympic gold for the sixth time in a row. Stars Tamika Catchings, Sue Bird, and Diana Taurasi each win their fourth gold medal.

GLOSSARY

assist
A pass that leads directly to a basket.

debut
First appearance.

intensity
Passion and strength.

point guard
The player who directs a team's offensive attack.

retirement
Ending one's career.

shooting percentage
The number of shots made divided by the number of shots taken.

triple double
Accumulating 10 or more of three statistics—usually points, rebounds, and assists—in a game.

TO LEARN MORE

To learn more about legendary women's basketball players, go to **pressboxbooks.com/AllAccess**. These links are routinely monitored and updated to provide the most current information available.

INDEX

Bird, Sue, 21–22, 25

Catchings, Tamika, 18–20
Cooper, Cynthia, 13–14

Delle Donne, Elena, 26–28

Edwards, Teresa, 8–10

Griner, Brittney, 26

Ionescu, Sabrina, 28–29

Jackson, Lauren, 20–21

Leslie, Lisa, 16–18
Lieberman, Nancy, 5–6

Miller, Cheryl, 6–8
Moore, Maya, 22

Ogwumike, Chiney, 28

Ogwumike, Nneka, 28

Stewart, Breanna, 25–26
Summitt, Pat, 8
Swoopes, Sheryl, 14

Taurasi, Diana, 22–23
Thompson, Tina, 14–16

Weatherspoon, Teresa, 10–11